RESEARCH METHODS AND STATISTICS IN PHYSICAL EDUCATION

BOOK FOR HIGHER EDUCATION EXAM, M.P.ED STUDENTS AND FOR U.G.C. NET/JRF EXAMS

SACHIN PATEL

DEDICATED TO

MY PARENTS

SHRI SARDAR PATEL

AND

SHRIMATI LALWATI DEVI

MY TEACHERS

Dr. PARDEEP KUMAR, Dr. SANDHYA TIWARI, Dr. J.P. BUKAR AND Dr. SARITA TYAGI

BROTHERS AND SISTER

ROHIT PATEL, MOHIT PATEL AND MANISHA PATEL

AND FRIENDS

SAHIL, ABHISHEK, AMIT, ASHISH, AKASH, SHAILENDRA, PANKAJ AND TAPESH

Contents

Preface

It gives me inmmense pleasure to introduce the book **Research Methods and Statistics in Physical Education** The book has been written strictly as per the need of research methods and Statistics for research scholars and M.P.Ed students.

A beginner needs to be introduced to basic concepts of research methods and Statistics. An attempt has been made to explain the same in a simple language and lucid manner.

It is sincerely hoped that both students ans teachers alike will find it useful and the present attempt will prove its worth.

I am indebted to all my family members for their support throughout my endeavour.

Acknowledgements

My special thanks to Dr. Pardeep Kumar, Dr. J.P. Bukar, Dr.Pushpendra Purushwani, Dr. Dinesh Parakash Sharma,Dr. Sandhya Tiwari, and Dr. Sarita Tyagi for providing the necessary suggestions, guidance and co-operation for the preparation of this book.

I would like to express my gratitude and extend special thanks to My Parents and Friends for empowering me to push my limits.

I would like to thanks my friends Aman, Satish, Deepak, Chandrakant, Sandeep, Akash, Atul, Sahil, Rohit, Pankaj and Umesh for always helping me in my hard times.

I would also like to thanks myClassmates for always supporting me.

At last, but not the least I would like to thank all of my former teachers especially Shiv Kumar Sharma Sir, Hema Tiwari Ma'am, Pawan Gautam Sir, Ritu Ma'am and Mahender Sir for instilling the quality to work hard and seek excellence in me.

CHAPTER ONE

Introduction to Research in Physical Education

Research is the systematic way of getting solution to a problem

- Systematic means step by step
- Every step should be executed as per its requirements
- Systematic and careful examination
- It is sometimes to fill the gap of knowledge
- To increase the stock of knowledge

Research begins with doubts, queries etc...... Research & Discovery both are different Discovery is a part of Research.

RE + SEARCH = RESEARCH

Finding out something again and again

Nature of Research

• *It is Systematic, Planned and Careful Examination*

- It is a Logicalprocess; every step has its own logics.
- It isEmpirical; based upon experience and experiment.
- It is Intensive(honest, Intelligent and exhaustive process)
- It is Reductive (Generalization of results) which leads to publishing the outcomes for the benefits of others. Making judgment of the true performance on the base of results of the sample, this is also called reductive.
- It is Replicable. (Some research can be repeat again and again). 100% repetition of work called replicable.

Meaning of Research

- Research is an attitude of enquiry.
- Research is a systematic solution of the problem
- The research is an honest, intelligent and exhaustive search for facts.
- Research repeated for several time it become principles, some principal repeated for several times it becomes theories. The same theories repeated for several time it becomes law.
- Creative work undertaken on a systematic way in order to increase the stock of knowledge
- It is to find out something again and again which is new or unknown to us.
- It is to find out the answer of any question
- It is to enquire about some method or something to gain knowledge
- It is know about the fact and reality

- It is a careful enquiry or examination in seeking facts or principles

Characteristics of Research

- Research is directed towards the solution of a problem (it means every research having a purpose)
- Research require expertise in its methodology
- Research demands accurate observation and description
- Research requires courage
- Research involve carefully designed procedure
- Research involves collection of new data from the first hand source or wins existing data for a new purpose
- Dissemination of results. (Publishing the r3esults at the end)
- Research emphasis the development of generalization principles or theories that will helpful in predictions future occurrence

Definitions of Research

Research is completely or extremely patience and inherent activity

Research is considered to be the more formal systematic & intensive process of carrying on a scientific method of analysis.

-John Vest

Any collection of data, information and facts for the advancement of knowledge -Martyn Shuttle Worth

Research is simply the process of arriving at dependable solution of the problems through the planned and systematic collection, analysis and interpretation of data.

-Strain Mouley

Research is the process of step use to collect and analysis information to increase our understanding on a topic or issue.

-Crew well

Research is a point of view on attitude of enquiry or a frame of mind not only for the critical purpose but an attempt to find out facts and face them ones they have been assemble

-Rusk

Research systematized effort to gain new knowledge

-Red Man & Mary

It is a prolonged intensive and purposeful search which includes scientific step of investigation to determine whether they fit to the formulated hypothesis. -Clifford Woody

Step of Scientific Method of Investigation

a. Formulating the problem (Research topic) or (Shape to the question) Situation of uncertainty leads to formulate the problem position of doubt in the mind help to develop the research problem. Asking a good question may lead to research problem, Hazy picture may help to develop an research question. A tangle (puzzle) yet to be resolved give an idea to research problem, thinking differently and Gap of knowledge
b. Delimiting the problem (setting the scope of the study)
c. Formulating the Hypothesis (Intelligent guess, tentative outcome)

Assuming the outcome of the research in the beginning of the problem

d. Selection of test and collection of data
e. Analysis of data while using appropriate statistics
f. Interpretation of data and formulation of conclusion
g. Test the hypothesis if it is accepted or rejected

h. Generalization of results
i. Dissemination (Publishing)

Unscientific methods of problem solving

a. Tenacity (Te-nec-ity)

It refers to believe in the absence of supporting evidence. It means the pupil develop or force to develop in a particular belief without having the proper logic in relation to the problem of or to get the answer of a question Ex: Rituals or Superstitious are the examples.

a. Intrusion

It refers to the self evidence in the absence of supporting logics, self experience.

c. Authority

Forcing the individual to the action or act
In this method pupil develop certain belief in absence of supporting evidences.
In sports, players develop a particular set of pattern and consider that pattern bring victory to them.
They afraid to break this pattern to avoid failure in to the life, similarly a coach or trainer wear a particular dress, blazer, tie, cap so that the winning luck will favor during the match, this tenacity as no place in science because they cannot develop the logical relationship between the game's outcome and their particular routine.

Intrusion knowledge is sometimes considered to be common sense of self evidence many self evident truths however are subsequently found to be false.

It refers to some authority how long been used as a source of a knowledge, although this is not necessary invalid. It depends on the authority and on the rigidity of adherence.

- Reductive method

In this method we derive knowledge through reasoning it is to relate the minor premise to major premise and finally draw conclusions.

Major premise is self evident, previously established truth or belief concerning a relationship and minor premise is a particular case is related to major premise
Ex: All men are mortal — Major premise The king is a man — Minor premise
Conclusion — The king is also a mortal.
Major- All basketball players are tall Minor- Rema is a basketball player Conclusion- Rema is also tall.

- Inductive method (Empirical method)

The word inductive denotes experience or experiment which is the key for collection of data. But, believing too much on our own experience has some drawbacks.

1. Our experiences are limited.
2. The retention of those expertise's also depends upon how the event agree with our experience and belief.
3. Our state of motivation to remember

Experimentations

Conducting experiments are also the part of inductive methods. The process of experimentation does not call scientific because of two reasons;

1. Formulation of hypothesis in the beginning
2. Verification of the hypothesis at the end.

Inductive methods are the part of scientific method of analysis but at alone doesn't called scientific investigation.
Classification of Research

On the basis of purpose research classify into two types;

1. Basic Research
2. Applied Research

Basic Research is also known as fundamental or pure research. It is the development of theories by broad generalization or tentative principles.

It is used for the sake of knowledge and not for the immediate field application. It is carried on animals as subject in laboratory situation.

According to Craver, Basic research is designed to add something to an organized body of scientific knowledge and doesn't necessarily produce results of immediate practical value in basic research once, knowledge is established it remain forever the other characteristics of basic research are as follows.

1. Discovery of basic truth and principles
2. Less attention on field application
3. Carefully controlled condition
4. Conducted in laboratories
5. Emphasis on accuracy and control
6. Use animals as a subject

Applied research

It is also known as field/educational research. The name itself implies or signifies the term applied reveals with relation with application Therefore it is a type of research which develop new theories not for the sake of knowledge but for the sake of immediate solution of the problem. The applied research generally deals with a second level of organization of knowledge which closing the gap between available knowledge and specific practical need in application. The other characteristics are

I. Immediate application
II Practical in nature.
III Involving in product and in process
IV. Limited control over the research setting
V. To address immediate problems
VI. Establishing relationships
Vll. Use human participants
Conducted in less controlled conditions/ real world settings
Animals as subjects
Human as a participant
Developing theories
Immediate solution for the problem
It involves process not product
It involves both process and product

Types of research

Every research in relation to human activity involves scientific methods of investigation but as per the task in different kind of problem different methodology is involved. It brief description of different kinds of research is given.

1. Descriptive research
2. Experimental research
3. Analytical research
4. Qualitative research

S. Mixed research

Descriptive means the status of a particular group or a population ex: Description of psychological and physiological characteristics of footballer

Description of the status of health of housewives of age ranging 30-45 yrs. Description of health related physical fitness of elementary school children Survey of health status of tribal girls

Generally for descriptive research the three techniques are commonly used

1. Questionnaire method
2. Interview method
3. Normative survey

Questionnaire

It is a set of questions based on particular characteristics and used to obtain the responses of the groups. Questionnaire always used in survey research the main, justification for using a questionnaire is the need to obtain responses from people belongs to wide range of geographical setting

Interview method

Interview method and questionnaire method are basically the same as far as the planning and procedure is concerned when the population is specific and less in no. the input technique is utilized to obtain the responded from the participants.

The survey involving,

- Arjuna awardees
- Vice chancellors
- National athletes

In this technique a series of questions is to be asked in a set of sequence. It means the sequence of questions should not be changed from one person to another person. In interview technique always have some advantage in comparison to questionnaire method

Normative survey

It generally used to gather performance or knowledge data on a large sample from a population and to present the results in the form of comparative standards or norms.

In normative survey

Example: the development of norms for health related physical fitness of Indian school children.

Norms are the performance conversion tables when the performance is converted into points.

Other descriptive research techniques are as follows

1. Case studies
2. Developmental research

3. Co-relational studies
4. Observational research
5. Epidemiological research
6. Job analysis

- Case study

It is used to provide detail information about an individual or institute or condition. This technique used widely in medicine psychology, sociology and counseling.

Ex: - Contribution of Dr. P.M. Joseph in physical education in India Contribution of Swami Vivekananda in reform in education system Performance of Milka Singh at International level.

- Developmental research: -

It is generally concerned with the interaction of performance or knowledge with the maturation

The study of growth pattern of height and weight in school children (5-10 yrs of age)

Two techniques are available in developmental research

1. Longitudinal technique
2. Cross-sectional technique

Longitudinal technique

In this technique the same participants or subjects are considered for assessment of performance at different stages of phase of performance.

In above example the data will be recollected when the children become S yrs old, 6 yrs old and so on.

Such technique requires more years to collect the data.

Cross-sectional technique

In this technique the same participants or subjects are considered for assessment of performance at different stages of phase of performance.

In above example the data will be recollected when the children become S yrs old, 6 yrs old and so on.

Such technique requires more years to collect the data.

Cross-sectional technique

In this technique the data will be collected in first instant while considering 5-10 yrs of aged children means in for above example.

SO subjects from each age group will be considered simultaneously

- Co relational research

The purpose is to examine the relationship between certain performance variable to the actual performance the actual performance is denotes as dependent variable and performance variable denotes as independent variables.

In every sport the overall playing ability is called as dependent variable where as performance associated variable or characteristics finding out such relationship b/w independent and dependent variable are concerned in co relational research where, cause and effect relationship will be developed.

Relationship of selected motor fitness components to the sprinting ability.

The relationship of selected physiological characteristics to the performance of swimmers.

- Observational research

It is a descriptive technique in which behavior are observed in the participants natural setting such as class room or playing environment in this technique the particular behavior will be coded in form of frequency and duration of particular behavior.

. Job analysis

It is done to describe the nature of a particular job including the duties responsibilities and preparation required for success in the job.

Sometimes it also includes the minimum eligibility criteria of a particular job.

- Epidemiological research

Such studies are concerned with the help fitness and safety concern

1. A survey of obese population among school children.
2. The survey of tension among working women.
3. The survey of postural deformities among school girls.
4. Survey of lipid profile among males of 45-55 yrs.

- Analytical research

As the name suggest analytical research involved in depth study and evolution of available information in an attempt to explain the complex phenomena.

They are as follow

1. Historical research
2. Philosophical research
3. Review
4. Research synthesis

Ex: - analyses of Drag push in hockey.

Historical-researchdeals with the events of the past it means those had been already occurred.

In such research the past event thoroughly examine and compare the present in the contest and add some extend predicting the future

In historical research the scholar traces the past event. Philosophical research

Critical enquiry characterize philosophical research it means the philosophical research mainly involve critical thinking on a particular context.

Ex: - development of curriculum, course content, syllabus, essential requirement and qualification are mainly dealt with philosophical research.

Such research involves vigorous criticism in the light of fundamental assumptions Vigorous criticism: - to see every aspect of making positive or negatives.

Reviews

It means the summary of past researches in relation to particular concept.

Suppose, a review on selected physiological variable to the sport performances in such case the research scholar go through all the competitive research mainly concerned with physiological variable and sport performances.

If on a particular topic 20 computed work is available analysis the outcome of every work on the basis of significant or insignificant results the scholar decides the common outcome of all the competitive research is called review (Analysis of the Analysis) Research synthesis:

It is a basic type of research which involves logical conclusion that leads to valid conclusions, hypothesis, evolution and reason of old theories or proposing new theory. It is also showing further direction to the researcher to conduct research in the new area. A good research synthesis results in several conclusions and increase interest of researches in the same direction.

• Experimental research

In experimental research the effort of certain stimulation to be measured while other factor efficiently controlled by the scholar. These stimulation are denote as independent variable whereas, it effect on the performance is considered as dependent variable. The efficiency of experimental research mainly concerned with how efficiently a scholar can control all other factors except experimental factor.

1. Effect of conditioning program on the physical fitness component of B.P.Ed 1st year boys.

In experimental research the effort of program can be efficiently measured in two steps.

a. Assess the performance before and after the training to calculate improvement in the performance.
b. Calculate the changes in the performance due to the other factors
c. Calculate the real changes due to the training program in the performance by neutralizing the effect of other factors.

It is systematic method of enquiry and there establishes hypothesis in the beginning of the study the researcher is prime instrument in data collection and analysis such research characterized by intensive 1Stand presences. (the researcher must present at the time of data collection) the test for data collection are observational method, interview method, and researcher designed instruments.

Quality always expressed in the form of expression in numerical values.

Need of Research in Physical Education

a. To make the progress in the field of human relationship.
b. To check the progress in the field of growth & development, physical, mental, social and emotional aspect of mankind.
c. To solve the problem through experimentation
d. To select best method and procedure of teaching and training
e. To save energy, time and money.
f. To know the individual potentiality and capacity
g. To improve the performance
h. To select the appropriate games and sports according to individual's body types.
i. To know the attitude of people towards health and fitness
j. To avoid injuries by developing protective gadgets
k. To select the best technique for better performance

Importance of Research in Physical Education

a. Increase efficiency with economical efforts
b. Research leads to adaptation of new methods
c. Research dignifies the work of the teacher or the coach.
d. It helps to bring sense of awareness.
e. It helps to know the facts
f. It helps to solve the problem with logical approach.
g. It helps in better understanding of teaching learning process,
h. It promote educational reform
i. . It helps to check the social behavior of an individual or a group.

j. It stimulates the athletes for better performance
k. It investigate new methods and technique for quick improvement.

CHAPTER TWO

Developing the Research Problem

Identifying the research problem

a. Locating the research problem
b. Criteria of selecting the research problem

The most important task for a researcher in the beginning is to select a problem. It is a fact asking a good question is the beginning of research. A good question leading to formulation of research problem can be asked only when the researcher has enough experience innovation and a sharp intellect dictionary defines "Problem" as a matter difficult for settlement or solution.

In research a problem in fact is a gap of knowledge or a situation which has no clear solution a picture which is hazy and tangle which is yet to be solved.

As an academic discipline and professional field physical education and sports offer a wide spectrum of problems form such areas as health fitness recreation training and competition performance, management and so on. For identifying workable problem and preparing their blue print involve a lot of work on the part of researcher.

• Locating the research problem

I.Analyze literature in an area or subject field like, medicine, management, engineering, health and fitness, games and sports, Economics, Social issue, marketing and so on.

ii. Analyze thoroughly an area of special interest in the field

iii. Systematically record of unsolved problems

IV. Study researches of unsolved problems

V. Study researches already completed in a particular area

vi. Inform himself or herself regarding the current research going on in the university.

vii. Examine controversial issues.

VIII. Consult with member of the facility.

IX. Discover interest of association and society.

- Criteria for selecting research problem

It is divided into three parts

- Personal criteria (Knowledge, exposure, Interest)
- Research criteria (is it possible to get the conclusion at the end)
- Social criteria (how much it is beneficial to society)

Personal criteria

Interest of the scholar is the prime concern ii. Adequate training and experience iii. Check the problem is within the capabilities iv. Check the problem is within the resources like participants, availability of test, and availability of statistical technique.

v. Personal gain means contribution and usefulness

Research criteria

Scope should be clearly demarcated (specific and definite) ii. Appropriate to get the solution of the problem iii. Is it possible to collect data iv. Availability of techniques of analysis

Feasibility in relation to time, money, energy and man power

v. Contribution in the field of knowledge or professional contribution or think of future.

Social criteria

Check the selected problem is valuable for the society (benefit for the society) ii. The present research must stimulates the future researcher and motivate people. iii. Check the problem is essential for the present situation iv. The selected problem should reveal truth without bias.

Hypothesis

Hypothesis is a supposed statement in tentative explanation, tentative organization of facts in a needful way to be tested it is considered as prime instrument in research and it give proper guidance to the research activity.

The term hypothesis derived from the Greek work is Hypo — means "less than or under" and thesis — refers to place or generally it means anything under consideration of it is less than generalization.

Hypothesis is a pre — position which is tested to determine its validity.

-Good and Hall

Hypothesis is a tentative assumption the validity of which remains to be tested

-Land Berg

It can be described by some of the following terms: -

1. Preposition
2. Assumptions
3. Intelligent guess
4. Provisional guess
5. Guess based upon experience
6. Tentative assumptions

Characteristics of Hypothesis: -

A good hypothesis possess the following qualities

1. Closest to observable things
2. It should be simple and have no complexity
3. The terminology used in the hypothesis must be clear
4. A good hypothesis should be practically tested.

S. The hypothesis should be relevant to the problem.

1. Hypothesis must be specific and should not be prove generalization
2. The hypothesis should be related to available techniques.
3. It should be fruitful for new discoveries.
4. It must have power of prediction.
5. Hypothesis must possess internal harmony and consistency

Importance of Hypothesis: -

1. Separating relevant from irrelevant observation

Ex: comparison of motor fitness of basketball and volleyball players.

2. It is to the point inquiry (exact) (only for the sake of that particular problem)
3. Selecting required facts

   (Basketball and Volleyball players in relation to motor fitness)

4. Provide direction to the researcher
5. Act as a guide
6. Provide link b/w theory and investigation
7. Provide link b/w assumption and observation
8. Save time, money and energy.
9. Help in development of research technique
10. Leads to proper conclusion.
11. Help for development of research.

Formulation of Hypothesis
A Hypothesis may be formulated through a number of its solutions
The followings main sources for formulation of hypothesis are as follows:

- Personal experiences
- Imagination & thinking
- Observation
- Scientific theory
- Previous study
- Culture

1. Personal experience of a researcher is a great source of hypothesis on the basis of his/ her personal experience they use their mind and suggest some points for eradication (removal) of a social problem through developing a good hypothesis.

   Greater the researcher experience leads to higher/quick formulation of hypothesis.

2. Imagination & thinking's:

Creative thinking and imagination of a researcher helps in formulating a good hypothesis. Personal idea and thinking capabilities of a researcher would lead to greater no. of hypothesis formulation as well as control over the problem.

3. Observation: -

One of the best sources of hypothesis is the key observation of the researcher. In consideration and undertaking a research problem observation is necessary.

The collection of previous facts and current facts related to the problem leads to formulation of good hypothesis.

4. Scientific theory

Theory is capable in explaining all the facts relating scientific theory to the problem.

Scientific theory is a feasible source of hypothesis formulation.

The theory which is used by a researcher may satisfy the needs of making hypothesis because the theory explains the known facts.

5. The findings of the previous study are also a source of developing a concrete hypothesis.

If a researcher used previous knowledge about a phenomena for a particular place then another researcher follow their techniques or formulate his own hypothesis.

6. Cultural

Cultural background of the community may also help in formulation of hypothesis

Ex: comparison of endurance between tribes and non — tribe people. We have to see the cultural background of that particular area.

Culture is the accumulation of ways of behaving and adaptation is a particular place

While formulating a hypothesis a cultural effect must be studied in relation to the problem.

If we want to study trends towards female education in a particular area for this purpose we should study tradition, family system norm, value, region and education system of that area.

Process of research

1. Locating the research problem
2. Criteria of selecting the problem
3. Writing introduction (to selected problem)

First few pages of information must be general to specific

- Statement of the problem
- Delimitations
- Limitations
- Hypothesis
- Definition and explanation of terms Significance of the study.

4. Review of related literature

For the purpose of proposal at least 10 review should write.

5. Procedure of methodology.

- Selection of subjects
- Selection of variables
- Criterion measures

6. Analysis of data and result of the study.
7. Summary, conclusion and recommendation.

Delimitation

The boundary of the study which is to be predetermined by the research scholar. It also exhibits the scope of the study.

In general terms, it may also call as demarcation of the study. Delimitations are the choices that the scholar made to define a workable research problem.

Ex: - "comparison of selected physiological variables among players of racquets sports" In the above statement 'selected' used for the followings:

Heart rate ii. Vital capacity iii. Positive breath holding capacity iv. Negative breath holding capacity

They all are workable

Delimitation includes the no. and nature of the subjects to be used as well as the number and kinds of variable Number-> How many (No. of subjects)

Nature-> Performance wise, category of population (male or female)

There are at least 4 major aspects of the study which requires demarcation at the beginning.

1. Geographical setting (the study confine to district, state, university, school, college, country and other regional based population.)
2. Sample characteristics (the characteristics of the participants like age, sex, gender, trained or untrained, athlete, non-athlete, subjects having special characteristics like players belongs the different games and sports, vocational characteristics, physical educationist, engineering, medical etc)
3. Nature and No. of variable

It may be confined to physical, anthropometrics, physiological, psychological, biomechanical, sociological, and bio-chemical.

4. The unit of measurement in each selected characteristics

It means in what unit of measurement the particular assessment is recorded.

Delimitation gives an idea about the effect and details of the study it avoid the vagueness or confusion which may be created due to the title of research work. It helps to the research scholar to keep the workable problem into an appropriate size. Hence less important concepts of things should not be mentioned in the title and such things must be presented under the headings delimitation in chapter one of research report.

"Relationship of Motor Performance to the Playing Ability"

Limitations: -

In behavioral research like physical education and sports, there are various situations which are not in the control of scholar. The effect produced by such situation is called as a limitation and must be described in the research report.

Limitations known as encroachment or influence in the results of the study along with the required independent variables.

Ex: The effect of weight training program on physical fitness of school going boys.

In this research topic the influence of motivation level of school children their daily routine, their rest, their diet, their extra participation in P.E. and sports program.

These factors must be mentioned separately in the thesis but whatever is possible must overcome and should not be considered as a limitation shrinking from the hard work and sincere effort under the pretence of limitation is no wisdom.

The mentioning limitations in the research report are also called as accepting the weakness of the research and sometimes it also refers to the dark page of the research report. The result of the experimental research may be affected due to several reasons and can be considered as limitations of the study the limitations are the followings, time and season of the experimental and physical state of the subject.

- Time and condition of sport and measuring equipments when during use
- Daily routine of the subjects (before and after the training session)
- Diet, Rest, Exercise and social stress

- Impact of previous studies in form of review of related literature.

Things come late in the knowledge of the research scholar and occurs suddenly during experiment data collection or new findings is published after that has become the solution case to indicate the extend at which this affect the present study and must be present in the limitation section

In the planning of research such short coming should be eliminated as far as possible in the planning stage and in case or measure problem the study should not continue. Stating the short comings doesn't save the investigator from

responsibility and the truthiness or the validity of the research work. It means more no. of limitations may consider as low valid study and vice-versa.

Significance of the study: (Contribution/importance)

1. To the development of theory
2. In relation to solve immediate problems
3. Adding something into the knowledge
4. Or fill the gap of knowledge

    - Most unavoidable question a scholar faces at the time of proposal meeting. As well as final significance of the study,
    - The question may be asked in any form but a scholar must answer in appropriate manner.

Therefore, most of the thesis format are involve this aspect in any one form of the followings: -

1. Needs of the study
2. Importance of the study
3. Significance of the study
4. Contribution of the study
5. Rational of the study

    - The significance of the study should dismiss the importance of the proposal research and its relevance.
    - The investigator must relate the outcome of the problem for theory, practical and future research.
    - He also explain its contribution for the advancement of knowledge
    - Significance of the study gives information on benefits of the present study.
    - The work of research study is judge largely by whether it is applied or basic research
    - Significance of basic research, focuses on extends of the study to contribute in the formulation or validation of same theory.
    - Whereas, significance of applied research depends upon its contribution to the solution of some immediate problem.
    - It is difficult to write by the fresher scholar because they think only in terms of practicability of the study That is how the result can be immediately to improve same aspect of the profession
    - Therefore, the significance section must focus in the followings.
    - Therefore, the significance section must focus on the followings: -

1. Contradictory findings of previous research
2. Gap in knowledge in particular area.
3. Contributions that the study might make to the users.
4. Difficulties in measuring aspects of the phenomena
5. Verifying existing theory.
6. Practical application.

CHAPTER THREE

Review of Related Literature

For selecting a topic it is necessary to review literature related to any present study, or to check (going through).

Reviewing of related literature is "Going through all relevant material in relation to the present study from various sources.

a. Library
b. Archery galleries
c. Historical museums
d. Internet

- Library is the main source, valuable source of reviewing literature.
- Picture, photographs, paintings, sketches. Equipments, physical remains, article.
- Site related to review of related literature

Purpose of reviewing research

In major part of developing research problem is based upon what has already been published about the problem many research may already have been done on the problem in which a researcher is interrupted whatever the topic the past researches are in valuable in the planning of new research. Review of relates literature is important to develop a more general explanation or a theory to explain certain phenomenon for the thesis the review will be more focused directly addressing the question and method for the study most frequently the researcher attempt to relate studies by similarities and differences in theoretical framework of problem statement methodologies and findings and finally the results are determine by counting votes.

In the beginning the scholar will not have a deep understanding of the published research in his/her field to acquire this knowledge is the aim of post graduate program once the problem has been outlined the next step is to examine the literature for the following purposes.

1. To identify properly the extend of the problem
2. To make sure that study has not been done before.
3. To develop hypothesis
4. To develop an understanding of various technique available for such study.
5. To interpret the findings of results.
6. To develop ideas that contributes to overall study.

These purposes can only be achieved by a systematic and through study of the research literature available at all the sources.

The survey of literature must be completed before the data collection the reasons are as follows: -

To make sure that study is properly formulated the major consideration have not been over looked and see to prevent duplication.

Thus should not be interpretable to mean that once the data collection gas began there is no longer any need to pursuit further studies research process is over only after exhausting all the available sources.

Moreover, during the month of data collection analysis and writing research report the other results of the similar nature may be published in the journal and must be acknowledged.

Need for Reviewing Related Literature

It should be clear that before processing formally with data collection the survey of related literature should be completed. It help the scholar in the following way: -

1. Determine, if the study has been already completed and published.
2. Determine, if a similar nature of study is in progress.
3. Discover research elite the problem.
4. It provides ideas theories, explanation and hypothesis valuable in understanding and formulating the problem.
5. It helps to understand research procedure and statistical application employed by other and statistical application employed by others.
6. It helps to locate comparable material useful in interpreting the results
7. It help in proper understanding of the significance of the research study.
8. It helps in preparation of the background of the written research report.

Types of Literature

The related literature basically divided into 8 kinds

- Critical literature (directly related with our problem)
- Allied literature (indirectly related)

Critical = centric in nature

Allied = peripheral in nature

Certain public studies that relates directly to the topic under investigation arel called critical to study as the name who suggests the topic studies those are centric in nature to the topic under consideration

Ex: - If the study involved the effect of decrease environmental temperature on muscular temperature of college age men. The literature critical to the problem would involves similar studies that have investigated the effect of cold on performance those that have been concerned with muscular endurance and those related studies that have been utilized adult male or on different sample characteristics.

Allied Literature

Allied literature involves those studies that are related to investigation but are more peripheral in nature than the centric in nature. They are also important because they form some concept to the study and they provide background upon which it res. In the same above example the literature allied to the study may include those studies that have been investigated on hot or humid temperature, conditions as well as executed with muscular endurance or explosive strength

When variables are same, same conditions and same age groups -> critical literature.

Justification and understandings of the test used:

When a scholar using standard test to measure particular characteristics does not require justification but if the investigator using modifies form of some test or new test definitely require justification for using this test. It will be better explained in form of mentioning it’s reliability, validity, objectivity, utility and feasibility.

Type of sources: -

There are two types of sources.

- Primary source (first hand information)
- Secondary source.

Primary sources

Information collected first hand of from such sources like historical document, artistic work, experiment, survey and interview it is the direct description of the study by the individual who actually observe the occurrence and carries it out.

The original studies or articles in research, journals, thesis and resultation are the primary sources. Secondary sources

It includes complication written by a person who was not a direct observer or participant in the event describes Books, Encyclopedia, References, reviews are the example of secondary sources. Steps in Literature Search

The research scholar should follow the six following under mentioned steps when reviewing the literature performing these steps and show toughness and make the research more productive

STEP 1

Write the problem statement

STEP 2

Consult secondary source

STEP 3

Determine the descriptors

STEP 4

Search preliminary materials STEP S

Read and record the literature.

STEP 6

Write the literature review

Write the Problem Statement

By carefully defining the research Problem the researcher can kee the literature search within the limits. The problem statement and hypothesis may change based upon the search write the statement as complete or concise as you can at this stage

Consult Secondary Sources

This step helps the research scholar to gain overview of the top but if the scholar having sufficient knowledge about the topic so then they can omit this step. Secondary sources such as book, research reviews, and encyclopedias are helpful when students have limited knowledge about the topic. The scholar can get the advantage from background information and a summary of preview research certain research reviews and encyclopedias

I. Research review:

Annual review of medicine

Annual review of psychology

Review of educational Research

Physiological review

Psychological review

Exercise and sports science reviews

2. Encyclopedias

Encyclopedia of sports science and medicine

Encyclopedia of physical fitness

Encyclopedia of physical education, fitness and sports

Encyclopedia of educational research

Encyclopedia of research or teaching

Educational research information center (ERIC.com) Determine the descriptors:

Descriptors in general meaning is keywords.

Descriptors are terms or words that help to locate sources pertaining to the topic.

For the given statement "the effect of student teaching on attitude towards teaching in P.E". Some examples of descriptors are as follows

- Student teaching practice
- Internship program
- Physical education
- Attitude
- Change in attitude

Search Preliminary Source/ Material:

Use general sources to find out primary source are the purpose of this step. This may be executed through computer added subjects. General sources mainly consults of abstract and indexes which helpful to researcher in P.E.

exercise, science and sports sciences.

Abstract

Concise summary of research study are called abstracts and valuable for source and information for researcher. It also includes summary of paper presented at national or international conferences.

Indexes:

Indexes mediciss

Psyc info

ERIC

Sports discus

There are the few indexes available at the computer searches and provide lot of secondary sources, Bibliographies.

They are the list of books and articles about the specific topics. A good research strategy is to look for the most recent sources of information and then watch backward.

Library information system

The traditional cards with little trace of cards containing bibliographic information by author and subjects as all but disappeared clearly all universe libraries have gone to a computerized catalog system in such case the researcher first select the type of research from a menu such as author title, keywords and number.

When the source is found the display for the reference includes author title and publication information until, unless a scholar familiar with the computer operation search process become much faster and more productive.

Computer search

Computer search facilitates or generally predicts the literature search. Automated searching may provide mass effective and efficient excess information in comparison to searching manually. The key to a successful literature search is careful planning of the search process. Therefore while planning the problem statement identify the related descriptors or keywords. Some data basis available for computer searches are as follows:ERIC (1966)

Medline (1966)

Psyc info (1967)

Sociological abstract (1963)

Resolution abstract online (1961)

Ingenta (1988)

Sport discus (1975)

Web of sciences (1965)

Adjusting the Scope of Search

To increase or decrease the scope of search the specific words are used these words are called Boolean operators.

These words are or, and.

Ex: suppose the item listed for attitude change is 2237. When using attitude and teaching item is 186

Using word students teaching attitude Using 'And' reducing the scope of the research whereas using 'Or' means increasing the scope of research.

Correctness and accuracy of information it is usually difficult to verify in fact much of the information may be wrong or misleading there are few sources available which verifies the accuracy of information these sources are scout report (http://scout.cs.wise.edu), SOSIG (http://sosig.ac.uk) and 1400/ the virtual library.

Read and Record the Literature

The scholar must read, understand and record the relevant information from the literature keeping in mind the information may be utilized at any time until the viva examination was conducted the following information must be recorded in case of developing abstract.

Statement of the problem

Hypothesis

Characteristics of participants/subjects

Instruments and test used

Testing procedure

Independent & dependent variable

Treatment applied to participants

Design and statistical analysis Findings

Question rose for further studies.

Citations to other relevant studies.

Record or Write the Literature Review:

After the researcher have to located and read the necessary information and record the appropriate bibliographic data. Now the scholar should write the literature the following information must be consider for writing the literature review

1. Title of the study
2. Nature of the study
3. Name of the author
4. Year of publication

Must be given in one sentence.

Ex: Clark and Clark (1985) conducted a study on 50 non-athlete college boys to see the differences with athlete boys

5. Name of independent or dependent variable along with its measuring tools. (Name of characteristics, name of variable and measuring test)
6. Mention the statistical procedure adapted for analysis.
7. Findings & Results of the study to be mentioned.

All together the total abstract should not be more than 10 sentences

CHAPTER FOUR

Formulating the Method

Method means procedure

Needs and importance of formulating the methods: once the introduction and review or related literature has been completed the scholar must describe the methodology for the research. The purpose of method section is how to explain, how the study was conducted. The standard rule is that description should be through enough for competent researcher the purpose is for to reproduce the study that is if anybody is using the same number, material and method should arrive at the same result.

Above concept is match with one of the nature of research that is replicable.

Further the following involvements make it consider for formulating the method.

1. Keep the study straight forward so that when scholar find something can understand and interpret what it means.

   Understanding the data is an important concept

1. To eliminate any other alternative hypothesis that mean that when a scholar design the study correctly and properly.

   Maximize to variants and minimize error variance.
   Describing participants:
   This section of method in thesis describes how and why the participant are selected and which of this characteristics are important to the study. The followings question must be consider while selecting participants.

1. Are participants with special characteristics
2. Necessary for research

   Can we obtain the necessary permission and operation from the participants?
   Can we find enough participants?
   The following special characteristics are to be taken into consideration for selecting the participants.

- Age (children, Youth, Elderly)
- Sex (male or female)
- Level of training (trained or untrained)
- Level of performance (national, university, school or advance, intermediate and beginner)
- Size (on the basis of body type, fat)
- Special type (athlete, swimmer, player of different sports and games)

In this case inform consent form must filled by the participant.
This form having two parts one is informed and second is consent.

Inform means the purpose and objective of the study to be explained to the participants and request the participants for cooperation.

The second part consent means the participants are agreed to take part in the study.

The no. of participants must be appropriate depending upon the nature of study. (Sufficient No.)

In experimental research the interaction among participants measures the nature of treatment program is essential in allowing the treatment program to have a change in the performance of significant improvement, of course the scholar want to select such participants those are self motivated towards the training program and its measuring.

Describing Instruments

In this section, information about the instrument, apparatus or test must be described by the scholar, which is used to collect appropriate data for the purpose of study.

The following points in relation to instrument must be described.

1. Validity and Reliability of the test or an instrument.
2. Mention the availability or source of such instrument from where obtained instrument.
3. The complete understanding of operational procedure of the instruments.
4. How the instruments are used to evaluate two participants performance.
5. It is possible to obtain reasonable range of score for the selected participants. (must provide different score for different performance level)
6. The time spent to collect individual performance should not be too high.
7. Adapt appropriate testing procedure to reduce overall time consumption.
8. Describe the name of manufacturer, model no. and specific characteristics of the instruments.

Describing Procedure

In this procedure section the scholar should describes how the data were obtained including all test and procedures for obtaining scores on the variable of internet. How test was given and who gave them are important features. The scholar should also detail the setup of testing situation and instructions given to the participants if the study is experimental in nature the scholar should describe the treatment applied to the different groups of participants.

(It means schedules of training programs)

For planning the treatment:-

The scholar must consider the treatment should how long, how intense and how often.

The scholar should see the response or reaction of the participants to the treatment or program.

How the scholar administer these program.

The scholar should decide the starting load of the training program (through the result of pilot study)

Procedure section must contain all the details to allow another researcher for replication of the study. Therefore, a specific order or sequence or steps must be mentioned along with the timings of the study, instructions given to the participants and finally briefing, deep briefing and safety and also other procedures.

Sampling Techniques

Random sampling

Stratified

Sequential

Purposive

Snow ball

Random sampling:

When the selections of subjects are from the population is based upon principle of sampling. The principle are-

- Every member of the population must get equal chance to select as the member of the sample.

- The selection of sample is based upon chance not on choice.

Drawing a lot by rotatory disc, rotatory drums and random tables are used in random sampling techniques.

Stratified sampling:

This technique is better than random sampling techniques because this overcome certain demerits of random sampling technique. In this technique the population is further subdivided into 2 or more than 2 categories on the basis of special characteristics with in the population such as age performance level academic standards participation level and so on.

This technique further sub divided into two parts

- Proportionate stratified sampling techniques (equal % from every level)
- Non- proportionate stratified sampling techniques (equal no. from every level)

Sequential Sampling Technique:

In this technique a particular system will be developed by the research scholar as for the requirement of size of sample. All the individuals in the population will be given in a particular sequence or no. and then as per the size of required sample a system will be developed

Ex: suppose in a population having 100 subjects every one of them given the sequence from 1-100. The required size of sample is suppose 10 then the system is $100/10=10^{th}$.

Purposive sampling techniques:

When the selection of subject is directly based upon the purpose of the research work

Ex: suppose a study is on interuniversity badminton players then all those represented interuniversity in badminton will act as a subject.

Snow ball sampling technique:

In this technique every subject of the sample is free to select another subject and can increase the size of the sample.

Describing design and analyze

Describing design is important mainly in case of experimental research where, progress or change in the dependent variable always associated with the type of training program. It stops the rise of alternative hypothesis with the help of good design the outcome will be described in much meaningful way.

Generally the design is a format or process to control the outcome of experimental research a design study is one in which the only explanation for change in the dependent variable is associated with the training program given to the participants while describing such things in method it helps the scholar to eliminate all rival hypothesis

Describing analysis

The plan of data analysis must also be reported at the end of method section the researcher explain the proposed application of statistics. Along with the level of significance in all the research report descriptive statistics such as mean and standard deviations are reported for each variable to understand variability of sports if a correlation technique is involved it also to be mentioned along with its formula.

If for experimental research, as per the no. of groups' appropriate statistics to be measured for example: comparing two groups- t test, for comparing more than 2 groups- f test.

CHAPTER FIVE

Ethical Issues in Research

The right ethics of conducting research is mainly the scientific way of problem solving in every aspect of research way of problem solving in every aspect of research honesty, truthfulness and transparency must be observed by the scholar. At any difficult stage in the process and overcoming this difficulty by unscientific way is called misconduct in research. At the foundation stage scholar must be aware issues related to scientific misconduct or dishonesty the final decision at every step is taken by the scholar even though various do's and don'ts are available.

Shore (1999)

Identify seven area of scientific dishonesty which might occur in the total process of research.

Plagiarism

The dictionary meaning of plagiarism is theft, piracy, infringement or appropriation.

It is an act or instance or using or closely imitating the language and though of other authors without authourity are the representation of that authors work as our own and not giving due credit to the original author.

As research plagiarism means using the ideas writing, and drawing of others as our own of course, this approach is completely unacceptable in the process of research. Plagiarism carries several penalties at all institute. A researcher may be banned even for life in his/her profession.

No potential outcome will work if it involves plagiarism. Never allow a paper with your name on it until unless you have been seen the complete paper in its original form.

In scientific writing originality is very important common practice is to circulate the draft of paper among scholar who is known to be working in the specific area. If ideas methods findings and so on borrowed from others proper credit should be given to the original author.

Fabrication and falsification

Fabrication means the act or process of fabricating and untruthful statement and falsification is to alter or to make incorrect or to represent falsely.

More than 40,000 journals publish during a year and involved many research article. Therefore it is not surprising the scholar occasionally caught making or altering research data it is all because of pressure on the scholar particularly in health related researcher because of the following reasons.

- Expensive
- Required external funding
- Involved risks
- Not getting sufficient participants The response of participants.
- Running out of time
- Getting shortcut and so on.

As per the American republic federation and plagiarism in proposing, reviewing, conducting research and in reporting research results (Federal Register October -14 — 1999)

Non — Publishing of data: - (not mentioning the raw score at the end)

The research scholar avoids including some data at the end of research report because they do not support the designed outcome. This tactics sometimes known as cooking data, bad data should be identified if possible at the time of collection of data.

Although extreme score can create problem in data analysis and training them automatically is poor practice during the time of data collection there the research scholar should prevent the raw score at the end of research report in appendix section.

Faulty data gathering

A. number of unethical situations can occur at the time of data collection of the research in particular graduate student should be aware of such issues. The issues are:

- Malfunctioning of equipments (not giving the correct reading)
- In appropriate treatment to the participant
- Continuing data collection from participants who are not meeting the requirements of research.

Ex: Poor efforts, lack of motivation, not concentrating on best performance, exhausted or so on.

Incorrect record of data

Poor data storage and retention

Data must be stored and maintained as originally recorded and should not be altered. These original records of data must be preserved and produce for examination federal agencies and most journals suggested that original data the maintained for at least 3 years from the publication of research.

Misleading Authorship

A. major ethical issue among researcher involves joint research projects more specifically the publication and presentation of joint research effort this should be based upon researchers contribution to the project the senior author is usually the e researcher who develop the idea and plan for research.

Second and third author are normally listed in order of contribution.

There are two rules which help to define authorship

1. Authorship should involve only those who contributes directly to the specific research project report
2. Technicians do not involve as a joint author

Unacceptable publication practices

The final deals of a research project is go for publication this point comes into picture when the publication between the professor and the graduate students. It is the duty of the professor to involve all the graduate students in major research program. The total result of the project should be published in one format in one journal

Generally good scientific practice is to publish all the appropriate data in a single primary publication researcher who do not follows these general type of rules may be viewed as lacking scientific objectivity in their work and lacking ethical issues in research.

Ethical issues regarding Copyright

Graduate students should be aware of copyright regulations and concept of fair use as it applied to educational materials. Copyrighted material is often used in thesis and dissertation This use is acceptable and permitted.

If the purpose is commercial then the use is unacceptable and researcher must seek the permission from the copyright holder and mention it appropriately

The concept of fair use has following basic rules: Purpose

Nature

Amount

Effect

a. Purpose

The purpose is educational or commercial consideration to be given to the educational purpose

a. Nature

It means copying is accepted or not copying a journal article for personal cite is excepted and is a violation of fair use concept

c. Amount

It means how much is copied (less or more)

d. Effect

How does copying affect the market for the document/for the book? Making a single copy of research article has little effect on the market of the journal but copying a complete book or chapter of the book reduces royalty to the author and income for the publication.

Therefore this act is not fair. Finally, it is advisable that before copying any material the scholar must seek permission from the copyright holder.

Responsibility of researcher

The following responsibility may be listed for researcher

- The researcher must have proper understanding and concepts for scientific dishonesty in research. Like, fraud, misrepresentation, inaccurate interpretation of data, plagiarism, unethical, obligation practice and so on While proceeding into the research process step by step must be aware of ethical issues
- Under such situation where decision to be taken it must support to good ethics Star, process and finish the research work as per the time availability.

Therefore time management is very important

- Try to get sponsorship or funding for collection of data, typing and printing research reports and purchase of other low cost equipments and data gathering materials.
- Findings it is decision of the research scholar to involve in unethical issues or not there are few other reasons of involving scientific dishonesty in research.

a. The need to complete graduation work with in time limit
b. Pressure of obligation (Govt. schemes like UGC)
c. To get timely promotion in higher education

Working ethics with Faculty:

Ethical factor in the student — professor relationship are important consideration. It is a desire of a teacher that their student should become scholar after completion of research work. Therefore teacher should treat graduate students or research scholar as colleagues at the same time graduate student must act like responsible scholar this means producing careful thorough and high quality work few consideration a scholar must keep in mind while selecting the supervisor.

- Must select as per their area of interest

- Don't choose in a hurry
- Carefully evaluate the specialization of the faculty and it should be in our interested area.
- Check the publication of faculty in the special area
- Read some of their publication and determine your interest
- Talk to the fellow graduate students to get the feedback regarding working style of the concern professor.
- Finally talk to the concern facility to determine or convince them to consider your name as research scholar under his/her supervision.

CHAPTER SIX

Introduction to statistics

Statistics:

The Science that Involves the Extraction of Information from numerical data obtained during the experiment or from a sample.

<u>Statistics Deals with</u>

1. Collection of Data
2. Organization of data
3. Analyzing of data
4. Presenting of data
5. Summarizing of data
6. Interpreting of data
7. Drawing conclusion from data

<u>Purpose</u>

A. To summarize and describe a set of data from research study
B. An objective basis for drawing conclusions from the data collected in research study.

Importance

1. To interpret scientific literature
2. Determine the scientific worth of tests.
3. To prepare report based on tests
4. To conduct research
5. To evaluate reports
6. To make conclusions

Type of Statistics

1. Descriptive Statistics

Describe characteristics of single group

1. Comparative

Describe characteristics of two groups

3. Relationship

Determine Relation between numerous human traits.

4. Inferential

Make generalization to the population from the sample data.

5. Predictive

Predicts from Known measurable qualities.
Method of stats
Which Design to Choose
Factors that playing a vital role in choosing design

- The aim of the study
- The nature of the phenomenon
- Reliable
- Ethical conduct
- Cost.

Fundamental characteristics of statistics

1. Express quantitatively not qualitatively
2. Sum of total expression
3. Single observation not form statistics
4. Stats collects for a definite purpose

Types of Data Sets

1. Population
2. Sample

Population have one or more specific characteristics.
Sample is the subset of the Population
Types of Measurements

a. Parameter : Numerical measurements using population Data Set
b. Statistic: A numerical measurement using a sample data set

Types of Data

1. Qualitative : Non-numerical characteristics (men/Women)
2. Quantitative: Numerical measurements (height/weight)

What are Variables?
Things that we measure, control or manipulate in research

1. Independent: That are Manipulated
2. Dependent: Only measured and registered

3. Extraneous: Not Independent but have potential to change dependent variables.

Measurement Scales

1. Nominal Data

   Can be qualitatively only, Data Value serves as labels, (75% Pass, Below= fail)

2. Ordinal data

   Can be qualitative and quantitative
   Data serves as labels have a natural meaningful order.
   Ex. Ranking of Teams

3. Interval data

   Quantitative there is a difference b/w values after the intervals (D.O.B., Temp)

4. Ratio Data

   Quantitative, comparative in two or more quantities (Height vs waist ratio)
   Methods of Data Collection

a. Census

   Collect measurements from the entire population

b. Sampling

   Choose sample from the population
   Method of Sampling

1. Random Sampling

   Sample chosen randomly from the population

2. Systematic sampling

   A system is developed to choose from population
   Ex. Every 5th person from roll no.

3. Stratified sampling

   Sample is chosen from population with same qualities in similar ratio.

4. Cluster Sampling

   Each individual is mandate to be chosen from each group but not in similar ration

5. Convenience sampling

Sample are chosen as per our requirements
Types of Scores
Raw -: Scores that are not treated with any statistical methods
Statistical -: Set of score that comes after statistical treated
Group –: raw score have been grouped
Single -: Means of Class intervals

CHAPTER SEVEN

Simple Basic Stats

Basic Statistics used are as follows-:

1. Frequency Table
2. Measure of Central tendencies
3. Measure of variability
4. Measure of association

So in this chapter we are going to cover the basic concepts of frequency table
Definition of Frequency Table
Is a way of summarizing a set of data.
Frequency Distribution
Range-:
Highest-Lowest value
No. of Class intervals-: (Min 10-Max 20)
Size of Class Intervals -: Range/No. of C.I.
Tabulation.

C.I.	F	d	Fd
26-30	1	2	2
21-25	2	1	2
16-20 (A.M.=18.5)	3	0	0
11-15	4	-1	-4
6-10	5	-2	-10

Fd= -10, n= 15, s.i. = 5

$$(A.M. + (\sum fd/N) * s.i.) = 14.7$$

Sample of Frequency Table

Class width -: diff between consecutive lower or upper class limit
Mid-point-: (Lower class limit + Upper class limit)/2
Cumulative frequency
The sum of class and previous classes.
Class boundaries: No. that separate the classes without Gaps.

(Lower class limit 2- Upper class limit 1)/2
Frequency histogram
Bar graphs that represents frequency data without any gaps in b/w the bars.
Frequency polygon
Line graph emphasis the continues change in data
Shape of Distributions:
Symmetric: data is symmetric if the right half of its histogram is roughly a mirror image of its left half.
Skewed: it extends more on one side, if it's in right side then its right skewed or vice versa.
Uniform: Equally distributed, if all the bars are of equal heights in histogram then it is uniform.

CHAPTER EIGHT

Measure of Central Tendencies

These are the Statistics used to represent the center of the study

1. Mean

   Most common measure of central tendency
   $\Sigma X/N$

1. Median

   That deviates the distribution in half.
   N/2 if Data is in even no.
   $(N+1/2)^{th}$ if data is Odd.

3. Mode: it is the most occurring frequency.

   <u>Method of Calculating Mean</u>

1. Mean of Ungrouped data

$$8, 6, 2, 9 = \sum X/N = 25/4 = 6.25$$

Mean of Ungrouped Data

2. Mean of Group data

C.I.	F	m	Fm
45-49	1	47	47
40-44	3	42	126
35-39	5	37	185
30-34	4	32	128
	13		$\sum fm$=486

486/13= 37.3

mean of grouped Data

3. Assumed Mean Method

C.I.	F	d	Fd
26-30	1	2	2
21-25	2	1	2
16-20 (A.M.=18.5)	3	0	0
11-15	4	-1	-4
6-10	5	-2	-10

Fd= -10, n= 15, s.i. = 5

(A.M. + (∑fd/N) * s.i.) = 14.7

Assumed Mean Method

For Ungrouped data ∑X/N
For Grouped Data ∑fX/N
For Assumed mean method (A.M. + (∑fd/N) * s.i.)
<u>Method of Calculating Median</u>
For Ungroup Data
N/2 if Data is in even no.
$(N+1/2)^{th}$ if data is Odd.

1, 7, 9, 7, 6, 8, 1

ungroup Median N = 7, so, (N+1)/2=4, So the 4th term is the median

For Group data

C.I.	F	cf
26-30	1	15
21-25	2	14
16-20 (L.L.=15.5)	(f)3	12
11-15	4	(C.Fp)9
6-10	5	5

L.L. + {[(n/2-cf)/f]*s.i. = 13

Median for group data

L.L. + {[(n/2-cf)/f]*s.i.

Mode

It is the most occurring frequency in the ungrouped data

For group data

3Median-2Mean = Mode

3*13-2*14.7 = 9.6

CHAPTER NINE

Measure of Variabilities and Measures of Association

Measure of Variabilities consists of the followings:

1. Range
2. Quartile Deviation
3. Mean Deviation/ Average Deviation
4. Standard Deviation

Quartile Deviation

Provides a spread of Middle, 25% and 75%

QD = (Q3-Q1)/2

For Ungroup Data

Q =N is even N/4

When N is odd (N + ¼)Th

10, 10, 15, 20, 75, 93, 127

N = 7, N+1 = 8, 8/4 = 2 so Q1= 2th term

For Q3 we have to multiply by 3. So it is 6.

Quartile of Ungroup Data

N = 7, N+1 = 8, 8/4 = 2 so Q1= 2nd term

For Q3 we have to multiply by 3. So it is 6th term.

So Q_D = Q3-Q1/2 = 6-2/2 = 2

For Group data

Q1 = 1 (N/4)

Q3 = 3 (N/4)

C.I.	F	CF
80-89	11	116
70-79	12	105
60-69 (L3=59.5)	(F3)15	93
50-59	20	(CF3)78
40-49	20	58
30-39 (L1=29.5)	(F1)15	38
20-29	12	(CF1)23
10-19	8	11
0-9	3	3
	N=116	

Table for Quartile of Group Data

Q1 = L1+ (((n/4)-cf)/F)*s.i.
Q1 = N/4 = 116/4 = 29
Q3 = 3(n/4) = 3*29 = 87
Q1 = L1+ (((n/4)-cf)/F)*s.i.
= 29.5+ (1*(29-23)/15)*10
= 33.5
Q3= 65.5
= Q_D = Q3-Q1/2= 32/2=16
Mean deviation or Average Deviation
Ungroup = Σ(X-M)/N
Group = Σfd/N
Standard Deviation
For Ungroup data
S.D. = $\sqrt{\Sigma X^2/N}$
Directly from raw score
$\sqrt{(N\Sigma X^2-(\Sigma X)^2)/N}$
For Group Data

$$\sigma = c \times \sqrt{\frac{\Sigma f_i d_i^2}{N} - \left(\frac{\Sigma f_i d_i}{N}\right)^2}$$

C = s.i.

Measure of Association
Correlation.
Highest=1 and Lowest=0
Coefficient of Correlation

$$r = \frac{n(\Sigma xy) - (\Sigma x)(\Sigma y)}{\sqrt{[n\Sigma x^2 - (\Sigma x)^2][n\Sigma y^2 - (\Sigma y)^2]}}$$

Pearson Correlation

$$r = \frac{\sum XY - \frac{\sum X \sum Y}{N}}{\sqrt{\left(\sum X^2 - \frac{\left(\sum X\right)^2}{N}\right)}\sqrt{\left(\sum Y^2 - \frac{\left(\sum Y\right)^2}{N}\right)}}$$

pearson Correlation

Spearman rank Order Correlation

$$\rho = 1 - \frac{6\Sigma\, d_i^2}{n(n^2 - 1)}$$

Spearman Rank order Correlation

Graphs shows Correlation

1. Negative linear correlation

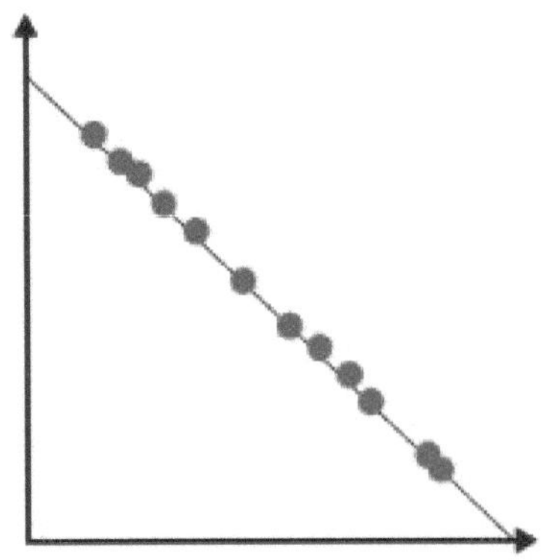

2. Positive Linear Correlation

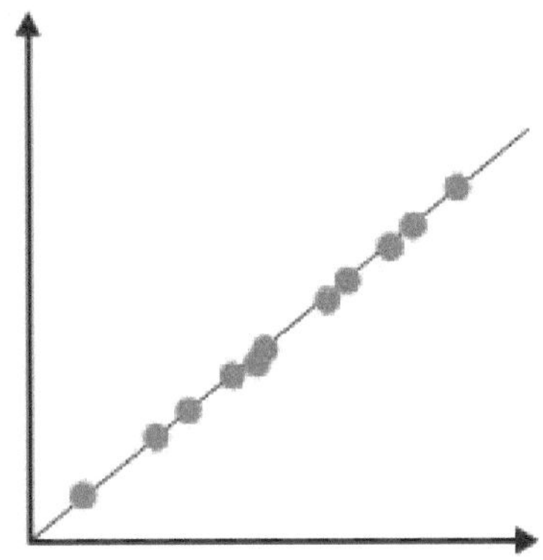

3. No – Correlation

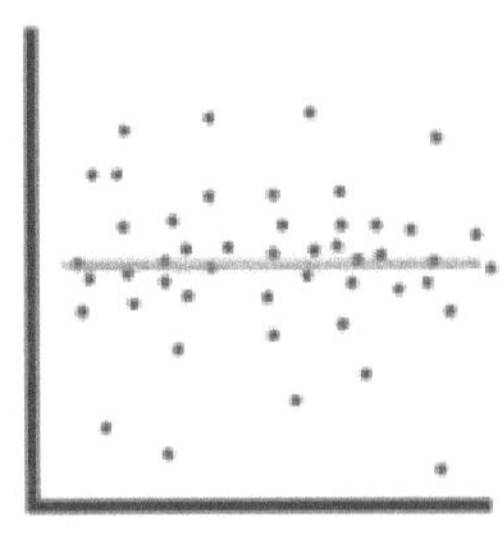

4. Non-linear Correlation

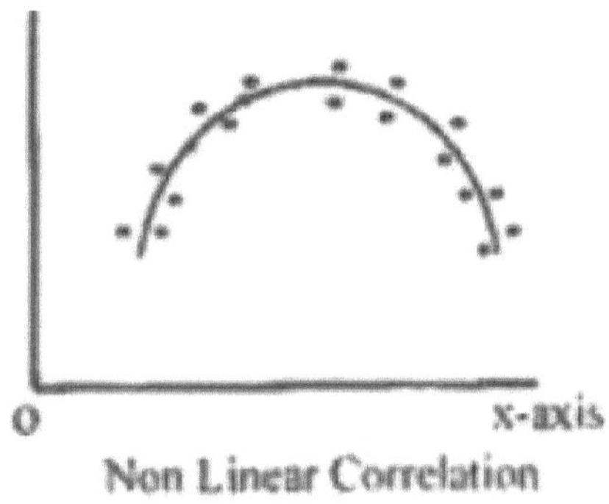

Enter Caption

CHAPTER TEN

Non Parametric methods, T- test and Anova

1. The test of differences between groups (independent samples)

1. Test of Diff. between Variables. (dependent Samples)
2. Test of Relationship between Variables

For Independent
We have two samples that we want to compare concerning their mean
T – Test (Independent)
Non- Parametric Alternatives
Wald-wolfwitz Runs Test
Mann- Whitney U – Test
Kolmogrov – Smirnov Two sample Test
If we have multiple Groups

1. ANOVA

Non-parametric alternatives Kruskal wallis Analysis of Rank and Median Test

1. If we measure two variable in same sample T-Test for Dependent Samples.

Non parametric alternatives
Wilcoxon matched pairs test
If variable of interest are Dichotomous in Nature (pass vs No Pass) Then McNemar's Chi square.
For Relationship b/w Pairs

1. Coefficient of Correlation

Non-parametric Alternatives

1. Spearman Rank order

If variables is in Categorical manner (male vs Female)

2. Chi square
3. Phi coefficient
4. Fisher Exact Test

Chi Square

Also known as test of goodness of fit

It was the statistic chi squared, X^2. Where invigilator check whether observed set of results matched on expected outcomes

Formula for Chi Square

$$\chi^2 = \sum \frac{(O - E)^2}{E}$$

O = the frequencies observed

E = the frequencies expected

$\sum$ = the 'sum of'

Example of Chi Square

Income Level

		Low	Medium	High	
Tax Bill	For	213 (209.9)	203 (187.2)	182 (200.9)	598
	Against	138 (141.1)	110 (125.8)	154 (135.1)	402
		351	313	336	1000

H_0 : voter's opinion concerning the new tax bill and their income level is independent

H_1 : voter's opinion concerning the new tax bill and their income level is not independent

Test Statistic: $\chi^2 = \sum \frac{(Observed - Expected)^2}{Expected} = \sum \frac{(O-E)^2}{E}$, where $df = (2-1)(3-1) = 2$

$$\chi^2 = \frac{(213-209.9)^2}{209.9} + \frac{(203-187.2)^2}{187.2} + \frac{(182-200.9)^2}{200.9} + \frac{(138-141.1)^2}{141.1} + \frac{(110-125.8)^2}{125.8} + \frac{(154-135.1)^2}{135.1} = 7.85$$

Critical Value: $\chi^2_\alpha = \chi^2_{(0.05,2)} = 5.99$

Sine $\chi^2 = 7.85 > \chi^2_\alpha = 5.99$ we reject the null hypothesis and conclude that voter opinion concerning the new tax reform bill and income level are not independent.

T - Test

Independent T test

$$t = \frac{\left(\overline{X}_1 - \overline{X}_2\right)}{\sqrt{\left[\frac{SS_1 + SS_2}{N_1 + N_2 - 2}\right]\left[\frac{1}{N_1} + \frac{1}{N_2}\right]}}$$

Formula for independent T test

Example

	Group 1	Group 2
	5	3
	8	5
	7	2
	8	3
	7	
sum	35	13
sum sq	251	47
N	5	4
mean	7.00	3.25
SS	6.00	4.75

$$SS_{Total} = \sum X^2 - \frac{\left(\sum X\right)^2}{N}$$

$$t = \frac{(7.00 - 3.25)}{\sqrt{\left[\frac{6.00 + 4.75}{5 + 4 - 2}\right]\left[\frac{1}{5} + \frac{1}{4}\right]}} = 4.52$$

ANOVA

1. One way ANOVA
2. Multifactor ANOVA
3. Variance Components Analysis
4. General linear Models

Example of One Way ANOVA

	G1	G2	G3
	3	4	9
	1	3	7
	3	5	8
	2	5	11
	4	4	9
	3	.	.
Sum of X	16	21	44
Sum of X^2	48	91	396
N	6	5	5
Mean	2.67	4.2	8.8
S.s.	5.33	2.8	8.8

We already know the formula for computing S.S.

df for Between K (No. of groups)-1 = 2
df for within N-K = 16-3 = 13

	df	SS	Ms	F
Between	2	108	54	41.4
Within	13	16.93	1.3	
Total	15	124.94		

9 798888 332689

Printed by Libri Plureos GmbH in Hamburg,
Germany